# CAN YOU BELIEVE IT?

## How to Spot Fake News and Find the Facts

Written by
**JOYCE GRANT**

Illustrated by
**KATHLEEN MARCOTTE**

For Val, a true friend. Thank you for believing in me. — J.G.

For mom & dad. Thank you for your continuous support. — K.M.

Published in Canada and the U.S. by Kids Can Press Ltd.
25 Dockside Drive, Toronto, ON  M5A 0B5

Kids Can Press is a Corus Entertainment Inc. company

www.kidscanpress.com

The artwork in this book was rendered digitally.
The text is set in Open Sans.

Edited by Kathleen Keenan
Designed by Andrew Dupuis

Printed and bound in Shenzhen, China, in 10/2021 by C & C Offset

CM 22  0 9 8 7 6 5 4 3 2 1

**LIBRARY AND ARCHIVES CANADA CATALOGUING IN PUBLICATION**

Title: Can you believe it? : how to spot fake news and find the facts / written by Joyce Grant ; illustrated by Kathleen Marcotte.
Names: Grant, Joyce, 1963– author. | Marcotte, Kathleen, illustrator.
Identifiers: Canadiana 20210199784 | ISBN 9781525303227 (hardcover)
Subjects: LCSH: Fake news — Juvenile literature. | LCSH: Media literacy — Juvenile literature.
Classification: LCC PN4784.F27 G73 2022 | DDC j70.4/3 — dc23

Kids Can Press gratefully acknowledges that the land on which our office is located is the traditional territory of many nations, including the Mississaugas of the Credit, the Anishnabeg, the Chippewa, the Haudenosaunee and the Wendat peoples, and is now home to many diverse First Nations, Inuit and Métis peoples.

We thank the Government of Ontario, through Ontario Creates; the Ontario Arts Council; the Canada Council for the Arts; and the Government of Canada for supporting our publishing activity.

# TABLE OF CONTENTS

# INTRODUCTION
## Gotcha! Spotting Fake News

Have you ever been fooled by a video or a news article that was really interesting but turned out to be untrue? You probably have — it's happened to us all.

Sometimes it's hard to know what to believe. Videos and posts on big, well-known news websites are usually trustworthy. But there are also lots of websites and **social media** accounts that post "fake news" — videos, articles or posts that contain exaggerations or lies. It can be pretty hard to tell the difference between what's fake and what's real.

For instance, guess which one of the **headlines** below is for a fake article:

**A.** VOLCANO SUDDENLY SPRINGS UP

**B.** NEWLY DISCOVERED EARTH-LIKE PLANET NAMED "ROSS"

**C.** PREVIOUSLY UNKNOWN BEATLES SONG FOUND IN LIBRARY BASEMENT

**D.** CITY LOOKING FOR VOLUNTEERS TO CUDDLE RABBITS

Maybe the weirdest thing is that three of those articles are *true*! All of them sound pretty unbelievable. But each one *might* be possible. And that's the key. Fake news often has a bit of truth in it, which can make it harder to spot.

Another thing can make fake news hard to catch: the way it's written. Real news is written in news style or journalistic style. People who write fake news often mimic that style, to make their lies seem real.

## Answer: Which Headline Is Fake?

**A. TRUE!** On February 20, 1943, at 4 p.m. in Dionisio Pulido's cornfield in Mexico, a 2 m (6.5 ft.) high crack suddenly sprang up from the ground! The Paricutín volcano spewed stone, ash and lava for nine years before becoming dormant.

**B. TRUE!** A planet about the same size as Earth was discovered in 2017. It's named after the star it orbits, Ross 128. And that star was named after its discoverer, Frank Elmore Ross.

**C. FAKE!** There's no "new" Beatles song. But it would be great if it were true. When fake news is about something we wish would happen, we may be more likely to be fooled.

**D. TRUE!** Cuddling helps rabbits and cats in animal shelters feel less stressed. More than 900 people applied to be animal cuddlers in Toronto, Canada, in 2017.

# Why Do People Write Fake Stories?

There are lots of reasons why people write stories that aren't true, and we'll talk about them later in this book. Some do it to boost the number of visitors to their website or increase their followers on social media. Others want to spread lies about someone or something. And some people do it to cast doubt about the real news, to get you to stop trusting any news **source**. That's a big problem, because people need sources they can trust for important information.

Unfortunately, fake news spreads faster than the truth. In fact, lies are 70 percent more likely to be shared on Twitter than real news, according to a 2018 study at the Massachusetts Institute of Technology (MIT). And when fake news makes you feel a strong emotion — anger, shock, confusion or even happiness — you're much more likely to like or share it.

Whoa! Everyone needs to be warned about this!

Sun to Burn Out Thursday

Wednesday

## What's the Good News?

It's possible to spot fake news! That's what this book is all about — what to look out for and how to investigate what you find, whether it's a video, a social media post or an article. And you'll go behind the scenes to see how real journalism works. Knowing how real news is made will help you become an expert at telling the difference.

Best of all, you'll be able to do it quickly. Who has time to spend an hour investigating everything they read online? The faster you can figure out that something's fake — and stop yourself from sharing it — the better.

Thursday

## What Is Fake News?

What exactly is fake news? Most of the time, it means shareable videos, articles and images that contain lies. (There are other kinds of fake news and they're covered in Chapter 4.)

Fake news is not a news article that someone just doesn't like.

Let's say Sam failed history. If an article in the newspaper said, "Sam Gets D− in History. Must Take Summer School," Sam probably wouldn't like it. But he can't say it's fake news, because it's true. Just because you don't like what you're reading, Sam, it doesn't mean it's fake news.

The key to figuring out what's fake is **critical thinking**. That means wondering about things. Being **skeptical**. Questioning what you're reading instead of just automatically believing it.

Fake news isn't going away anytime soon. But once you know what to look for, you'll be able to spot it — and help stop it from spreading.

Friday

# CHAPTER 1:

## Real or Fake?

It's easier than ever to publish information and get people to share it. People can just write whatever they want and post it online. It's quick, cheap and pretty easy. In fact, you can create a free website in less than an hour — and social media is even faster. And then, in theory anyway, you could make up anything you want, post it, add a photo and call it "news."

Lots of people do this. Many articles, videos and posts contain information that isn't true. But why would people do that? That's the million-dollar question. (And usually, the answer is money.)

**Click News Today** shared a link.

## You'll Never Believe What Happened When These Fuzzy Ducklings Escaped!

# Fake News, Real Money

Ads, clicks, likes and shares can all make money for the person who owns the website. Here's how: companies pay to put their ads on websites and the website owner gets that money. How much? Well, that depends on how much **traffic** (how many viewers) the site has. The more people who visit the website, the more money the website owner can charge for each ad. In 2016, news agency NPR reported that some fake news creators make up to half a million dollars a year. (Before you run out and start a career in fake news, remember, you'd literally be telling lies for a living. Not worth it!)

The website owner creates articles or videos that sound super interesting and then posts them on social media with an exciting headline, like "You'll Never Believe What Happened When These Fuzzy Ducklings Escaped!" An exciting headline gets people to click the link to find out what happened to those sweet baby ducks. When they click, they get taken to the website, which increases its traffic.

And by the way, nothing much happens to the ducklings. They quack and run around or whatever, but certainly nothing as exciting as the headline suggests. Fake news creators usually don't care very much about the reader — they just want that click. So, it helps them when we click on, like or share their fake news. It puts money in their pockets.

# I'm So Cool!

To get followers, some people use social media to make their lives seem more glamorous or exciting than they really are. They may even lie. Chances are, they want to become an "influencer" — a social media celebrity. Lots of influencers are simply experts or entertainers who don't publish fake news. But some do, and there can be money in it.

Let's say you're a celebrity chef with a million followers on Instagram. A lot of people will see what you post. Now, let's say a company that sells blenders gives one to you, or even pays you money, hoping you'll say nice things about it online.

Even if you hate the blender, you might give it a positive review, for the money or more free products. That fake news may persuade your million followers to buy a blender that you don't even like.

There's nothing wrong with influencers, but don't forget that many are paid to promote products. In fact, some have admitted they haven't even tried the products or have made false claims to make themselves look good. Some only post about products they truly believe in, but others are just in it for the money.

# The Nasty Side of Fake News

There are other, more dangerous reasons why people publish fake news. Some do it to get people to like (or dislike) a person or group or to influence an election. Lots of lies were posted online before the 2016 U.S. presidential election. For instance, a lie that Pope Francis wanted Donald Trump to become president was shared more than 960 000 times on social media. There is evidence that Russia spent millions of dollars spreading fake news before that election and others. Why would one country care who's president of another country? One possible reason is that countries do business together — they buy one another's products and services. So if you're a leader of a country, you want people you *like* to get elected in other countries. They would be more likely to do business with you and help make your country richer.

Some people spread lies about a group or organization they don't like in order to get others to dislike them, too. Hatred and racism are behind some fake news. Someone who is racist may take a random photo of a racialized person — maybe from their Facebook page — and add a fake headline suggesting they're doing something bad.

Racism probably makes you pretty angry, and it should. Fortunately, there's something we all can do to help. When you're reading something online, stop and think before you like or share it.

Cleaning up the internet won't happen overnight — but it won't happen at all unless we all work to stop it.

# Let's Get Real

Real news articles usually have some features that fake news doesn't have. For instance, real news articles typically have a **byline** that names the person who wrote the article. And photos on real news articles usually have a **photo credit** that says who took the photo or drew the illustration. Fake news articles often don't have either of those things. The publisher may be using the words or photos without permission. Or the writer may not want anyone to see their name on something fake. Sometimes, they'll make up a name, like "Jane Smith." But you can find out if Jane Smith is a real journalist — just search the name and see what else she's written. Does it seem legit? Investigating the *source* of news can be a good way of finding out whether it's real. The illustration on this page shows you some other features of real articles. You'll learn more about how real news is made in Chapter 2.

While fake news can be cheap and easy to publish, real news is expensive. You have to pay a news team to gather facts and check them. Also, lots of real news can seem kind of dry and boring. That's because the mission of a news organization is to give facts and information, not create excitement.

## REAL NEWS

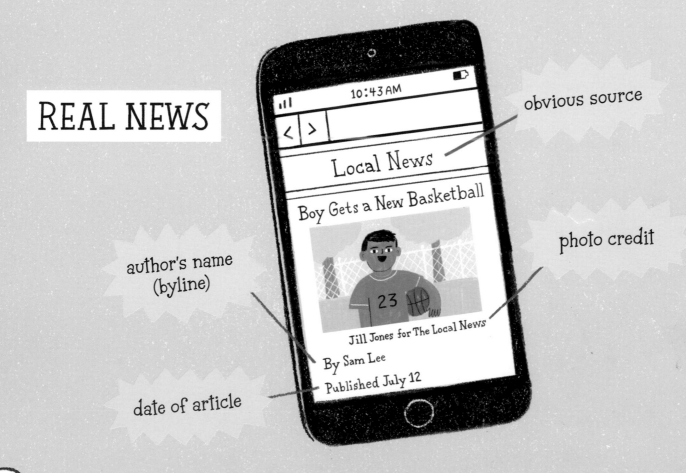

obvious source

photo credit

author's name (byline)

date of article

10:43 AM

Local News

Boy Gets a New Basketball

23

Jill Jones for The Local News

By Sam Lee

Published July 12

# How an Ordinary Basketball Can Make You Popular

If you can make information more interesting — **sensationalize** it — with an exciting headline or photo, then people are more likely to click on it and share it. Just like with the basketball example below, exaggerations or lies can make something that's ordinary more exciting. So an over-the-top headline that promises the extraordinary? It may not be real. (And yes, sometimes real news organizations publish sensational headlines, too. It can be hard to tell just from a headline whether something is real or fake — that's why you need to investigate.)

## THE TRUTH: INTERESTING

## NOT TRUE: MORE INTERESTING

## REALLY NOT TRUE: SUPER INTERESTING

# CHAPTER 2:
## The Good Stuff

Once you know what *real* news looks like, spotting the fake stuff will be way easier. Real news is written in news style. It's as **unbiased** as possible and doesn't exaggerate. It gives the basic facts: WHAT the story is about, WHO is involved, WHEN, WHERE and WHY it took place and sometimes HOW things happened. Not every news article will include all of these five Ws (and H), but journalists keep them in mind so the reader gets enough information — facts — to understand what happened.

Journalists put the most important facts first in a story. That's to give people the information they want as quickly as possible. It's also why newspapers are divided into sections. Don't want to read about sports or fashion? You can skip right to the section you do want.

# Don't Bury the Elephant

What are the "most important" facts? It depends. Let's say you're telling your brother what happened at school. "Hey, John! We watched a movie in history class. I got an A on my science project. I saw an elephant walk down Main Street. I scored three goals in soccer."

What would your brother say? "Wait! You saw an *elephant*?"

In journalism terms, you've "buried the **lede**." A lede is the most important information and it usually comes first. In this case, that would probably be the elephant (assuming you live where elephants on the main street are rare), but that fact is buried way down in your story.

It's important to put the most important fact first, because not everyone will read or listen to every word. If you give them the information that's most important to them right away, then even if they stop reading or listening after that, they've gotten what they need.

Once you've identified the elephant as your lede, you would then choose the second-most important fact, depending on who you're talking to. Journalists think about their audience and give them the facts they would think are most important. For instance, if you were talking to your parent, you might still want to lead with the elephant but follow up quickly with your A.

**2:16 PM**   localnews.com

# Elephant on Main Street

By John Duncan

Monday, May 17

An elephant walked down Main Street today just after 4 p.m.

"It was very exciting," said Kathleen Duncan, an A student and soccer player who saw the elephant on her way home from school.

Photo by Kathleen Duncan

# Talk, Read or Go

There are three main ways reporters gather facts for an article. They can

1. interview experts who know about it,
2. read information about it (from a book, website, study or poll) or
3. observe the thing or event themselves.

Journalist Jon Wells, at the *Hamilton Spectator*, calls this "talk, read or go." Let's see how this would work, using a fictional (made-up) train accident.

"Journalism, at its most basic, is about sharing important information, about politics and science and business, with a broad audience, and that's why it's so important for journalists to pay attention to details. Getting it partially right means you're not doing justice to the story."
— Freelance journalist John Lorinc

# Breaking News: Train Derailment

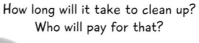

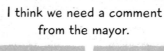

downtown-news7.com

## Oil Spill Cleanup Underway

By Leni Gotlib | August 23

Dozens have been forced to leave their homes after a train derailment and small fire this morning. About 250 barrels of oil leaked from one of the train cars, but the city's fire marshal says there is no danger to residents.

"Crews will remove the cars and then tackle the cleanup of the oil," said Mayor Ella Floyd. "It should take about a week."

*Photo by Greta Muller*

# Accuracy Is Everything

All reporters have the same mission: to gather facts and tell people about them. Often, an editor will give the reporter an assignment or story idea. The reporter does research and conducts interviews to get the facts. She may interview just one or two people, or many, as she chases down facts for her story. For all journalists, accuracy is the most important thing — by far. It's even more important than being the first to report the news.

"The credibility of the content in the *Globe and Mail* on all platforms rests on solid research, clear, intelligent writing and maintaining a reputation for honesty, accuracy, objectivity and balance."

— the *Globe and Mail,*
Editorial Code of Conduct

ON AIR

Once the reporter writes the article, an editor checks it for accuracy and to make sure the reporter has gotten the whole story. Later, a copy editor goes over it again for spelling and typos, and, at some news organizations, a **fact-checker** confirms the details are accurate. A photographer may be sent out to take photos. A headline is written and the article is posted on the website and social media. Later, it may also be published in the newspaper or magazine.

Reporters who work for radio and television stations and online media also do interviews. They record their conversations and then edit them. Those are also checked and double-checked for accuracy. Some broadcast reporters write articles, some go on camera (or produce videos) to report the news and some do both. Most journalists also post information on social media.

# Check It Out!

When reporters read something online or get a quote from an expert, they double- and triple-check the information by finding other solid sources that agree the fact is correct. For instance, if someone tells a reporter, "The moon is made of blue cheese," the reporter might do some research online and contact an expert at NASA. If the reporter uncovers contradictory information, especially from an expert, they will be very skeptical about that "fact."

# There's Always an Angle

There are lots of ways to write a news article, and every journalist (and their editor) must decide what the most important facts are. In the elephant article on page 15, for instance, the movie was left out entirely. Maybe it wasn't important enough, or the opposite: maybe it will be a whole other article.

After a journalist has gathered the facts for an article and decided which ones are most important to their readers, they will decide on an angle for the story. Since journalists almost never have room for every fact they've gathered, they also have to decide what to leave out.

The best way for readers to be sure they get the "whole story" is to read news from lots of different sources that have different points of view and audiences. If you're always getting your news from social media, for instance, try a mainstream media organization like National Public Radio (NPR) or the Canadian Broadcasting Corporation (CBC). If you hardly ever look at posts that aren't about sports, search for #politics or #music. And we should all make sure we're consuming videos, posts and articles by people from communities and countries other than our own. Soon, your news feeds will become more diverse and much more interesting — and you'll be better informed.

When a major international event happens, watch how different media cover it. They'll each have their own angle, depending on who their audience is.

Toronto Star

Canada Beats U.S. to Win Gold

NY Times

U.S. Nabs Silver in Spectacular Race

Buenos Aires Times

Argentina Makes Semi-Finals for First Time Ever

Beijing Daily

Chinese Athlete Scores Personal Best

nature.com

The Science Behind the Olympics

# Reporters Are Curious!

In an interview, the reporter asks questions to get facts. Here are some interviews you can try:

• Interview a friend about something that really bugs them.
• Interview an older person about the weirdest thing that ever happened to them.
• Interview a teacher about advice they would give to their younger self.

Reporters try to avoid questions that can be answered with yes or no, like "Do you have a hobby?" Instead, they ask open-ended questions, like "What do you do in your spare time?" or "Tell me about your favorite hobby." They listen carefully to the person's answer and ask follow-up questions like "Trick skateboarding sounds fun. Where do you do it?" Or "What's the coolest trick you've ever landed?"

# CHAPTER 3:

## Whoops! Mistakes Happen

No one's perfect, and sometimes reporters make mistakes. When they do, their website or publication publishes a **correction**. That's a small article or paragraph explaining the mistake and giving the correct information. While correcting something is good, often the correction isn't seen by as many people as the original error was — which is why reporters try so hard to avoid errors in the first place. Note that a "mistake" is not the same as **biased** or unethical reporting, which all media are sometimes guilty of doing. You'll learn about that in the next chapter.

## Good Catch!

Each year, the Poynter Institute for Media Studies publishes some of the wackiest corrections from various news sources. For example, when nine-year-old Alex Flores caught a massive 19 kg (42 lb.) blue catfish in 2019, the Associated Press (AP) ran a story about the impressive catch. Flores said he'd even named the fish "Whale Lord" — or so the AP reporter thought. Here's their correction:

"This story corrects a previous version to say the boy named the fish Wailord after the Pokémon character, not Whale Lord." Whoops!

"When we run a correction, clarification or editor's note, our goal is to tell readers, as clearly and quickly as possible, what was wrong and what is correct. Anyone should be able to understand how and why a mistake has been corrected."
— Corrections policy, the *Washington Post*

## Admit It, Fix It, Don't Do It Again

When a mistake happens, most news organizations:

- Find out what the true facts are.
- Publish a correction as quickly as possible, in the same place the error was made. If it was on Twitter, correct it on Twitter.
- Make sure it doesn't happen again. An editor may speak with the journalist to find out why the mistake occurred and create new guidelines so it doesn't happen again.

In 2018, the *New York Times* published more than 4100 corrections. The *Toronto Star* published more than 1500 corrections in 2019. This may sound like a lot of corrections, but remember, these publications print lots and lots of articles — in 2018, the *Times* published more than 55 000 stories, and in 2019, the *Star* published more than 30 000.

Oh no! That's not their name!

Whoops!

## What Happens on Social Media Stays on Social Media

If a mistake is made on social media, it never goes away. Online posts quickly get liked and shared. So even if the original post is deleted, someone probably has a copy. Reputable news organizations correct mistakes and let people know what happened and why. Corrections are made to articles, photos, artwork, videos, live broadcasts, audio clips and social media posts — all mistakes, no matter how small, need to be corrected in the same place they happened.

# How Do You See It?

Fake news is full of lies. But when is something "a lie" and when is something "the truth"? It often depends on your **point of view** — how you see things and what's important to you. For instance, let's say your hockey team had a massive win and you knocked another team out of the playoffs. If your stepmom asks, "How was the game?" you'll probably say, "Awesome!" And it was awesome — for you. But what about the kids on the other team? They probably don't think the game was all that awesome. From their point of view, it sucked.

In a conversation like this, no one would really expect you to answer on behalf of the other team. But journalists have to think about everyone who is involved in a news event — not just the people they know or who are most like them. They have to try to look at the news from multiple points of view.

## Missing the Point

It's impossible to include everyone's point of view in every news article, but there are some points of view that seem to be left out more often. People of color, the LGBTQ+ community, women and others who aren't male, people with disabilities and Indigenous people — their perspectives may be missing from news reports. As readers, we need to notice when an article doesn't mention an important point of view, possibly because all of its sources are from people with one specific cultural background. And we need to make sure to get our news from sources that include different perspectives.

# Why Are Points of View Left Out?

Every journalist has their own point of view, usually based on how they grew up and the experiences they've had. Their friends and contacts — the people they interview — may also have a similar point of view. If a news organization hires only people who have the same background, the points of view of people from other backgrounds could easily get left out of the story.

Not so long ago, newspapers in North America hired mostly white male reporters. People from marginalized communities, through no fault of their own, had a tough time getting hired. That is known as discrimination. Many news organizations are now making progress hiring journalists and editors from different kinds of backgrounds, but most newsrooms still aren't as diverse as their readers.

When limited points of view are represented in the news, it's not only the people in the stories who are negatively affected — it means that some people's stories won't get told. Readers may miss out on some really interesting and important information. Some people's voices will never be heard, or will be heard less often and less loudly than others'.

# Facts Aren't Good or Bad

Sometimes, a reporter's personal opinions about something affect the way they write their news article. This is called biased reporting. A bias is a prejudice in favor of or against something, based on personal opinion. Everyone has opinions, even reporters. But in news articles, reporters should be as unbiased as possible and give the facts, without adding their opinion. For instance, an unbiased statement is "The New York Yankees clinch the World Series." That same sentence, written by a super-fan of the Boston Red Sox, might read: "The New York Yankees got lucky (and probably cheated) to win the World Series." In this example, the reporter clearly hates the Yankees and wants you to dislike them, too. It's important for readers to watch out for bias and try to get their news from different sources so they get the whole story.

Rare White Anaconda Found Unharmed in Woman's Bathroom

Pro-Snake Bias

Hideous Snake with Huge Fangs Terrorizes Woman

Anti-Snake Bias

Actual Event

Ssstick to the facts.

# News Bias Is Nothing New

Many of today's news organizations have a political bias, or favor one political party over another. For instance: Liberal or Conservative, Democrat or Republican, left leaning or right leaning. Those biases are deeply rooted in history. In the 1800s in North America, newspapers acted as the voice of specific political parties or politicians. They printed news *only* from that party's or person's point of view. Totally biased! You had to read the other side's newspaper to get a different point of view.

## What Kind of Reader Are You?

Every news organization has a target audience. They write for a certain type of reader who wants to read about certain things. For instance, readers of *Sports Illustrated* like sports. If *Sports Illustrated* suddenly started reporting on the latest trends in teen fashion, their readers would be understandably confused. There are times when points of view are deliberately left out and that is appropriate.

# CHAPTER 4:

## Not Quite Fake, Not Quite Real

So far we've looked mostly at news, which is based on facts, should be unbiased and is double-checked for accuracy. But news is just one type of information that's online. In between news and fake news is a whole range of "news that isn't news."

### TEACHING KIDS NEWS

Opinion

**YOUNG PEOPLE ARE BEST EQUIPPED TO CLEAN UP THE INTERNET**

By Joyce Grant
September 15

# Opinion

Sometimes, articles are written specifically to persuade the reader to agree with the writer's point of view. They're known as **opinion pieces**, columns or editorials. They include the writer's opinion and have a *deliberate* bias that's obvious and not hidden. An opinion piece will often have the writer's name and photo on it, or include a link to their website, so you know who wrote the piece.

# Satire

Some "news" is meant to make you laugh. It's known as **satire**. It could also be called a spoof, a parody or a lampoon. Satire exaggerates or twists the news to make it funny. Sometimes, satire uses humor to point out something the writer thinks is wrong or needs to change. Here's an example:

# Man Who Remembers to Bring Cloth Bag to Grocery Store Twice a Year Declares Climate Change "Solved"

It sounds like a real news headline and it makes you laugh because no one really thinks that just using cloth bags a few times will fix a massive, worldwide problem like climate change. Using humor, this headline makes an important point — that doing little things makes us feel good as individuals, but much more is actually needed to really fight climate change.

Satire is often a good way to engage in difficult topics that some people don't want to think about, according to Trevor Noah, host of TV's satirical *The Daily Show*. In 2019, he told *The Guardian*, "You're using comedy to get into their brains."

While that's true, in the end satire is comedy — not journalism. Unfortunately, people sometimes fall for satire, not knowing it's a joke, because it can look like real news. Professional satire, like you find on *The Onion*, *The Beaverton* or *The Daily Show*, is very open about being comedy. Usually, it will label itself as comedy on the website's **About page**. While satire can be pretty funny, it shouldn't be anyone's main source for actual news.

# Advertisement (Ad)

To sell a product or service, companies buy ad space in a publication, on a website or in a video to talk about how great their product or service is and why people should buy it. Ads don't have to be unbiased. In fact, they're very biased — in favor of their own product. Ads are not news, and it's important to understand that they won't give you both sides of the story. Advertisers do have to follow certain regulations. For instance, they're not allowed to say their product can do something it can't. But they don't have to tell you all the bad stuff, either — things it doesn't do well or how superexpensive it is.

EVERY KID'S FAVORITE TOY

## SMOOTH ROCK

DURABLE! DOESN'T STAIN! HEAVY!

Throw it, catch it, let it fall.
Smooth Rock lasts forever!

Just $19.99

Coming soon: Smooth Rock 2.0

# Advertorial

This is an ADVERTisement that looks like an editORIAL. Don't be fooled — it's still an ad, paid for by the company that sells the product. Sometimes, advertisers try to make their ad look just like the news articles in the rest of the publication or on the website. They want you to think their ad is actually another article. But there are telltale signs. **Advertorials** often include a logo, a little image that represents the company. They may also have the word *advertisement*, *promoted* or *sponsored* on them (often in teeny tiny letters). Once you know something is an ad and not a news article, you'll also know that the information is very biased toward whatever is being advertised. That's why it's good to take the time to think about whether something is an ad or not.

Smooth Rock Is Versatile, Durable

"It will outlive me," says eight-year-old Jaya Misri.

SMOOTH ROCK

*Sponsored by Rock Labs Inc.*

# A Hippo ... in Your House?!

It looks like a normal hippopotamus, except it's the size of a mouse — what could be cuter? The house hippo lives inside people's kitchens, where it feeds on chips, raisins and toast crumbs. Wait ... what?

In 1999, a video that looked and sounded like a real nature program showed this strange little animal scuttling across the floor. Is there really such a thing as a house hippo? Nope. Special effects made a normal-sized hippo look tiny, and all the "facts" about the animal were completely made up. The video was created by a nonprofit organization whose aim was to help young people think more carefully about what they see and read. In 2019, the digital literacy organization MediaSmarts created an updated version, showing the tiny hippo playing with the family's smartphone and tablet. Cute — but not real.

POW!

WHAM!

# Clickbait

"You won't BELIEVE what happened to Melvin!" That headline makes you want to click on it, right? That's clickbait. The headline is like the worm on a hook, tempting you to bite.

But the article or video probably isn't as exciting as you thought it would be, and you'll notice you have to keep scrolling past a lot of ads to read or watch it. And that's really the point of most clickbait: to get lots of people to see as many ads as possible. Don't share clickbait unless you think it's something other people will actually want to read.

Which Superhero Are You?

BOOM!

ZAP!

BAM!

# Propaganda

**Propaganda** is a type of fake news that is usually about politics or world events and is very misleading. Propaganda hides its intention: to use lies to try to get you excited or angry about something. For example, during the COVID-19 pandemic, there was a lot of propaganda urging people not to wear a mask in public, even after it was clear that wearing a mask was one of the most effective ways to stop the spread of the disease. Many fake news posts made inaccurate claims, like "Wearing a mask lowers your oxygen level," "Masks don't block COVID-19 particles" or "The government makes you wear a mask to control you."

# Deepfake

A **deepfake** is a video that makes someone look like they said or did something they didn't. Deepfakes use **artificial intelligence (AI)** to mash together two videos: usually a person from one and a voice from another. It can be very hard to tell a deepfake from a real video, especially as the technology improves. Signs to look for include blurriness around the mouth or jawline (where someone else's mouth has been superimposed) or mouth movements that don't match what's being said. You can also search for key words from the video to see what reliable news organizations have said about it. But perhaps the most powerful thing you can do is be skeptical and think critically about what the person in the video is saying. Would that person really say those things?

Abolish the Monarchy!

**Conbren Terrance**
*@conbrenterrancium*
Male. Likes nature. Lives for life!
Joined October 2014

## Are You Following a Bot?

There are millions of bots (automated accounts) that post things on social media. How can you be sure that the "human" who's posting isn't actually a robot?

- Check the profile. Bots typically don't give their city or other personal information that can be verified.
- Bots have a tough time with language. They repeat themselves and may miss obvious jokes or sarcasm.
- No posts about hobbies or friends? Bots don't have personal lives.
- Do a reverse image search of the profile pic. And if they don't have one at all? Another giveaway.
- If they have only one follower or are mostly followed by other bots, that can be a sign.
- Fixating on one topic or putting up a post every few minutes could mean the account is automated.
- You can also check the username with a bot-checking website to see if you get a positive ID.

As you know, humans do some wonky things online — including some of the stuff on this list. But add a dollop of skepticism about the content of the posts and you'll have a pretty good recipe for avoiding bot-created content.

# Chameleon News

Take a look at how the same set of facts can be presented as a news article, clickbait, an opinion piece, an ad and an influencer's social media post.

## Just the Facts:

- Rani Kumar is in grade six at Valley Public School in Bloville.
- Rani enjoys skiing.
- Fifteen students submitted science fair projects, and eight of them got an A+.
- Rani's project came in fifth at the science fair.
- Rani wanted to test a fourth type of ski wax, Super Sticky Stuff, but she couldn't afford it.

**News Article**

yourlocalnews.com

### Rani Gets A+ on Science Project

**by Chadwick Jones**                    **March 14**

"I couldn't afford more than three waxes," says Rani Kumar, a grade six student at Valley Public School in Bloville, Indiana. She's referring to her science project "Does Ski Wax Work?" which earned her top marks this year — an A+. Kumar compared three waxes: Wacky Wax, Slippery Glop and Slip 'n' Ski. "Of the three waxes, Wacky Wax came out on top," says Kumar. "But expensive Wacky Wax came in second to just polishing our skis with a cloth. Cloth was the best, according to my data."

*Photo by Riley Chiu*

**Clickbait**

Scientist Spreads Sticky Gunk on Two Boards — And You Won't Believe What Happens Next!

Click Here

34

# Elbow Grease Beats Ski Wax
Ric Arnell, Columnist, Skiing World Magazine

People today spend too much money on expensive products. Take ski wax, for instance: a child at my son's school took top marks with her science project comparing various waxes. Do you know what worked best? Just polishing the skis with an ordinary cloth. And good, old-fashioned hard work doesn't have packaging that will ruin the environment.

WACKY WAX WORKS!

WACKY WAX

WACKY WAX

Ski Faster! Guaranteed!

## If you ski, you need Wacky Wax!

Its patented slippery-slide technology lets you ski down hills faster. Just ask scientist Rani Kumar: "Wacky Wax came out on top!" Compared to other brands, Wacky Wax works best!

*Just $19.99*

gord_downhill          ...

gord_downhill

I'm gorgeous Gord Downhill, gold medal–winning Olympic skier. If you want to be an amazing skier like me, you have to use Super Sticky Stuff! A scientific study by scientist Rani Kumar proved that it's the best ski wax in the world. And it's delicious on toast! Buy it!

35

# CHAPTER 5:
## Become an Investigator

So how can you tell when something's fake? First, be skeptical. And then be *more* skeptical. Don't take it at face value — question it!

In 2016, researchers at Stanford University did a study to find out how well young people were able to tell the difference between fake and real news. Let's skip right to their conclusion: not well.

That's not surprising, since fake news can fool adults, too. But there is one thing that adults tend to be better at than young people: being skeptical. (That's probably because adults have simply been alive longer than kids, so they've seen more things. They've probably been fooled in the past, so they know a bit more about what to look out for.) Skepticism is one of the most useful skills for judging whether online information is credible, according to fake news expert Sam Wineburg, who was involved in the Stanford study.

According to the study, when young people read something online, they tend to think it's probably true. That's okay if you're always getting your information from sources you know are credible. But if you're just scrolling through the internet reading random articles and posts, you need to be a bit skeptical.

# You'll Never Believe Which Headline Is Fake

It's especially important to be skeptical when an article makes you feel emotional. For instance, you should definitely think twice if a story ...

grosses you out:

**MUST-TRY TREAT OF THE SUMMER: SLUG-SLIME ICE CREAM!**

makes you outraged:

**BOYS NO LONGER ALLOWED TO OWN CATS: GOVERNMENT**

makes you feel super smart:

**Kids Are Better than Adults at Everything, New Study Shows**

is extra exciting:

**Teachers Agree: No More Homework, <u>Ever</u>**

sounds too good to be true:

**CHOCOLATE IS BETTER FOR YOU THAN VEGETABLES!**

seems ridiculous:

**UNICORNS DISCOVERED IN CENTRAL PARK**

makes you confused:

**PENCILS BANNED BY GOVERNMENT. "ONLY PENS FROM NOW ON," SAYS MAYOR**

makes you furious:

**Mean Man Snatches Candy from Baby**

is shocking or scary:

**Antarctica Sinking — Gone by April!**

A headline that makes you feel worried or confused or scared isn't necessarily fake news. But if you also have the feeling that something about it "just isn't right," then you should definitely be skeptical and investigate it to see if it's real or not.

# A Drop of Truth Can Sweeten a Lie

Fake news creators know that a lie is more believable when there's a bit of truth mixed in with it. That's because the author gains your trust with every grain of truth, so you're more likely to believe the whole story — including the lie. For example, check out this headline: "Zach Faye Cancels Autograph Session to Help at Homeless Shelter." Let's say it is true that a famous gamer named Zach Faye recently canceled a public appearance. Since you know that's true, you might also believe the reason — to help his community. What a great guy! Thanks to that fake news, people won't know the real reason he left those fans in the lurch: to go skydiving.

When some of the things in a video, an article or a headline are true, it's a short leap to believe the rest. A drop of truth sweetens the lie.

# If It Makes You Feel Super Smart, It Could Be Fake

Some stuff online makes you feel really smart. Take a headline like "Only 1 in 100 People Will Know the Answers to This Quiz." And then you answer all the questions right! You must be the 1 in 100. But guess what? They made the quiz really easy. And it's not true that only 1 in 100 people could answer it correctly. (Try asking a few of your friends to take it as well and you'll see.) If there's a headline or an article that makes you feel like you're the only one who knows something, you should probably question it.

Another example: articles that make you think a politician is totally bad — or totally great — and you knew it all along. For instance: "Our Terrible Mayor Has Done It Again!" Or "Our Wonderful Mayor Has Done It Again!" Depending on how you feel about the mayor, either of those headlines could make you feel smarter than everyone else. "I knew it! She screwed up — as usual!" Or "Of course she did something awesome! She always does the right thing!" (The truth is, political leaders aren't all-bad or all-good. They're just humans who have opinions that may or may not be the same as yours and who sometimes make mistakes.)

# Woman Trains Raccoons to Steal Candy

POLICE DEP.
26452

A woman in Clermont, Ohio, was arrested on Tuesday after police found more than $250 000 worth of candy in her apartment.

Police chief Hannah Toll said Heather Confection, 82, had trained local raccoons to break into her neighbors' homes and steal their candy, then drop it off at her apartment.

Confection saw the rodents rummaging through her garbage. After gaining their trust, she trained them to steal, said Toll.

"There were 36 animals stealing for Confection," said another police officer. The officer said Clermont police received many compliants from kids who couldn't find their Halloween candy.

"We caught the raccoons carrying bags of delicious candy on video," said Toll.

Confection's apartment was littered with wrappers and candy worth $25 000.

Raccoons have a sweet tooth. "Who doesn't love candy?" said one scientist, who asked not to be named.

Confection has been charged with theft over $5000. A charge of animal cruelty was added after it was discovered she was leaving the racoons only the disgusting candy corn.

She trained raccoons to steal?

Ali

 The police got the rodents on video.

Bennett

Wait, is a raccoon even a rodent?

 How would you train one? They're smart, but they're still wild animals.

Why would the neighbors let a raccoon wander around their house?

 Wouldn't the raccoons just eat the candy?

$250 000 worth of candy? A quarter of a million dollars?

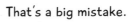 Near the end it gives a different number: $25 000.

That's a big mistake.

# Trust Your Gut

Some things in this article are making Ali and Bennett think, "Hey, wait a minute."

And that's good. Because if something on the internet makes you say, "Wait ... *what*?" you should question it. Trust your gut instinct — it's your first line of defense against fake news. Here are some other things to question:

- How did the raccoons get in and out of people's homes?
- Why would someone train raccoons to steal candy when there are other things that would be more valuable?
- The money mix-up is a big mistake. Are there others?
- Who is the unnamed scientist? What are they an expert in — candy or raccoons?

There are some true things in the article. There is a lot of candy around on Halloween. Clermont County, Ohio, exists. "Animal cruelty" and "theft over $5000" are real charges. Raccoons *are* smart and pretty good with their hands. Those real facts make the rest more believable.

# CHAPTER 6:

# And Now for the Good News!

Do you remember the first time you crossed a street on your own? You could have gotten hit by a car. But does that mean you should never do it? Of course not! You just need to learn how to do it safely. It's the same with the internet.

There is a lot of great information online that helps, entertains and informs us, and lets us connect with other people. It's hard to imagine being without the internet. But we need to learn how to use it safely. Being able to spot fake news will help to make the internet safer and more reliable for everyone.

zapatopi.net

## Help Save the Tree Octopus!

Soon, there may be no more tree octopuses! Wouldn't that be terrible? Logging, climate change and house cats are causing this creature's numbers to dwindle. This eight-armed animal could be headed for the endangered species list. One day, when we look up into the trees, we may not see any octopuses at all. Let's save the tree octopus! Click <u>here</u> to find out more.

Uh … hold on a minute.

A website, zapatopi.net, wants us to believe it. They posted information about the tree octopus and even a video of it. The site's About page is convincing. And there are links to other sites with tree octopus information.

But something's just not right. You're probably wondering: How could it breathe out of water? What would it eat? Why have I never heard of it?

You're right to be skeptical, because the tree octopus doesn't exist. The website is a hoax, created in 1998 to get people thinking more carefully about what they read. Like you did.

# Think Big to Find the Fake

Checking a website's About page and looking for .org (instead of .com) in the domain name are two things that used to help people spot fake news. Today, fake news sites can use just about any domain they want, and they can write anything on their About page. Instead, it's better to think critically about what you're reading. Ask yourself these questions:

1. Does something just feel "off" about it?
2. Does it make you extra emotional?
3. What's the source — who posted it and why? Are they reliable?
4. Have any well-known news sources reported it?

You're probably getting really good at spotting fake news. Now, let's take it up a notch. Turn the page for some advanced tips that will help you recognize fake news faster and more easily.

# Break the Fake

The more you investigate fake news, the faster you'll be able to spot it. Eventually, you'll be able to identify fake news within minutes — or seconds. You may not always be right, but even those few seconds may stop you from sharing something that's fake.

One of the most important times to stop and think before sharing is when there's *breaking news*. That's when something big or significant is happening (like a natural disaster, for instance) and events are still unfolding. People are quick to post big news on social media. They want to tell everyone what they've seen and heard. However, many of the earliest posts will contain information that isn't accurate. It's important to wait and allow "breaking news" to unfold and more information to emerge and be put in context before sharing facts that may not be correct.

# What Do Fact-Checkers Know?

In 2017, scholars at Stanford University gathered three groups of expert researchers: 10 historians (who do a lot of research), 25 students (who know a lot about using the internet) and 10 fact-checkers (whose job is to figure out if information is accurate). They showed each group two websites and asked them to decide which one had more reliable information. Most of the students got it wrong. About half of the historians thought both sites were okay. But every single one of the fact-checkers figured out which site was fake — and did it quickly.

What did the fact-checkers do right? They *left* the website. The students and the historians stuck to the site and were often fooled by well-crafted headlines, links and logos. The fact-checkers, however, looked quickly at the site and then Googled key words from it. They found out who had created the site and checked them out.

Another thing the fact-checkers had was "click-restraint." They scrolled through a page or two of search results and carefully selected only the most relevant articles to read. The top results of a Google search don't necessarily have the best information.

## Make a List of Credible News Sources

One of the easiest ways to avoid fake news is to have a list of excellent, reliable news sources you trust, such as well-known news companies or sources you've thoroughly investigated. Include all different kinds of sources so you're getting news from multiple points of view.

When you have sources you trust, you can use them to check news you suspect might be fake. If it's an important-sounding story but your trusted sources haven't covered it, it could be fake.

# Are Dog Lovers Dumber?

Now that you know how to spot fake news, let's see how Ali and Bennett do with this article that may or may not be fake.

theharold.com.co — □ X

## Dog Lovers WAY Dumber Than Cat Lovers: Study

An international study of people who love <u>dogs</u> has found that they are 10% dumber than people who love cats!

"Cats are just better than dogs," said researcher Dr. Leonard Spock.

Twenty people particpated in the study, which was printed in the *New Brunswick Journal of Nonsense*. They were asked a series of questions to find out how smart they were. Cat lovers scored seven out of 10, but dog lovers only scored six out of 10.

"Six out of 10 is pretty lousy," said another researcher.

"It's clear from the study that anyone who owns a dog should just get a cat instead," said Professor J. Humbug, an export on cats.

Fake, fake, fake!

I agree.

 The headline's silly.

Why is WAY in capitals?

 No byline or photo credit.

"Particpated"?

 Yeah, but I've seen typos in real articles.

There's other stuff, too.

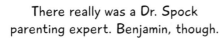 Dr. Leonard Spock ... sounds familiar.

There really was a Dr. Spock parenting expert. Benjamin, though.

 Yeah, and LEONARD Nimoy played Spock on *Star Trek*!

So, based on facts ... sort of.

 What's an "expert on cats," anyway? I mean EXPORT! Another typo.

We should look up *New Brunswick Journal of Nonsense*. Real or not, it sounds hilarious.

 They only interviewed 20 people. Is that enough for a real scientific study?

Dog owners should get a cat. That's weird advice.

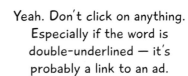 One or two of these things would tell us this article isn't real. But all of them put together ...

Yeah. Don't click on anything. Especially if the word is double-underlined — it's probably a link to an ad.

Don't feed the fakers!

# CONCLUSION
## Critical Thinking Really Is Critical

Having excellent critical-thinking skills will help you spot fake news, no matter how good it looks. To sum up this entire book ... here's what to do before you like or share anything online.

BREAKING NEWS
Oil Spill Cleanup Underway

EVERY KID'S FAVORITE TOY
SMOOTH ROCK
DURABLE! DOESN'T STAIN! HEAVY!
Throw it, catch it, let it fall.
Smooth Rock lasts forever!

Just $19.99

Coming soon: Smooth Rock 2.0

1. Question it. Be skeptical.
2. Ask yourself if something's just not right.
3. Is it trying to spark a big emotional response?
4. Have other media covered the story?
5. Check the source. Who posted it? What do you know about them?
6. Check out the author, photographer and people quoted. Are they real?
7. Do a search to see what others are saying about it.
8. Try a reverse image search (like a keyword search, but for images). Has the original image been altered?
9. Check the date. Is it old?

BLEND
-O-
MATIC

BLEND
-O-
MATIC

ALL-STAR
BASKETBALLS

PLAY LIKE
LEBRON

SUPER STICKY
STUFF

It's great
on toast!

SUPER STICKY
STUFF

BREAKING NEWS
Elephant on Main Street

## What Can You Do About Fake News?

If you spot fake news, don't click on it, like it or share it. If it's obviously fake and doesn't seem harmful, then you can probably just ignore it. Some sites let you block or "mute" people so you no longer see their posts. If you think someone has posted something that may cause someone harm, you could tell a trusted adult. They can report it and it may get investigated or taken down. Most social media sites, like Twitter, allow users to click a button to report harmful or abusive posts or bots.

NEWS
TEAM 5

# Is It Fake or Real? You Decide

Now it's time to practice what you've learned! Do you think this article is fake or real? How would you find out?

teachingkidsnews.com

## Loyal Dog Waits for Owner Outside Hospital

By Joyce Grant
Friday, January 22

Boncuk, a sweet little mixed-breed dog, finally has her owner back.

She had been waiting patiently outside a hospital in Turkey for the past six days, where her owner was being treated. Every day she arrived at the hospital about 9 a.m. and was taken back home every evening.

Her owner, Cemal Senturk, had been taken by ambulance to the hospital for treatment of a brain embolism. Boncuk escaped from the apartment and followed the ambulance to the hospital.

*Photo by Yara Uçar*

Since then, she managed to escape each day, to keep vigil on the steps outside the hospital doors. Senturk's family isn't sure how the dog managed to get out each day.

Hospital staff petted and fed the pooch, even providing it with a little mat to sit on.

Boncuk and her owner were finally reunited on Jan. 22, after Senturk's successful treatment.

 Does something seem off about it?

 Maybe ...

 Does it spark a strong emotion?

 Yes — I'm tearing up here. What a sweet dog!

To investigate further, you decide to look up some details.
We've listed below the results of your internet searches:

**You searched:** Where did Senturk live?

**Result:** It turns out his apartment is close to the hospital.

**You searched:** Vigil (meaning)

**Result:** Vigil: to wait quietly

**You searched:** Boncuk hospital

**Result:** 107 000 results, many news articles and videos, including *The Guardian*, Associated Press (AP), CNN and YouTube

**You searched:** Boncuk (meaning)

**Result:** Turkish: bead

**You searched:** Source: teachingkidsnews.com

**Result:** A kid-friendly news website that has been around since 2010

Here's a story that starts off with two suspicious factors: it sparks a strong emotion and it all seems a little too good to be true somehow. A dog that commutes each day?

You may have even wondered how the dog managed to break out of her apartment. (Maybe it's even bringing back vibes of the fake candy-stealing raccoon story on page 40 or the tree octopus website on page 42.)

But the story has a byline and photo credit and the website it's on is legit. And your internet search turned up many news media that had covered the story, including sites you trust, as well as video footage. It's starting to look more like a real news story, isn't it?

As far as we know, this story is TRUE! Anything's possible, so there's a tiny chance that all these news media were fooled and the story and video were staged … but that's looking very unlikely at this point. And one more piece of good news: these are techniques you can use whenever you're reading something online.

Now that you're an expert on spotting fake news, you can stop it in its tracks. And better yet, you can train others. If we all work together, maybe someday the only things left on the internet will be the good stuff! (You know: cute animal videos and real news.)

# AUTHOR'S NOTE AND SOURCES

Thank you for reading this book and for caring about journalism, facts and the news.

For more than 11 years, I've been publishing kid-friendly news on TeachingKidsNews.com to make the news more accessible for young people. I get to meet with thousands of students every year to talk about journalism. More and more, our discussions turn to misinformation and "fake news" and what kids can do about it. And that's why I wrote this book.

As you know by now, "critical thinking" is key. Asking the big questions: "Who created it? Why?" and most important, "Does this make sense?" No matter how tricky the fake news creators get, thinking critically will help us to sort fact from fiction.

The internet is an amazing tool. It connects us, informs us and entertains us. I'm not going to let the "fake news" makers stop me from using and enjoying it, and neither should you. Working together and doing some of the things in this book — like thinking before we click — we can make the internet better and more reliable. Believe it!

# TRUSTWORTHY SOURCES

## Websites

- Ad Fontes Media: www.adfontesmedia.com
- Civic Online Reasoning: cor.stanford.edu/
- Common Sense Media:
  www.commonsensemedia.org
- For the Record:
  www.classroomconnection.ca/for-the-record.html
- The International Fact-Checking Network
  (Poynter Institute): www.poynter.org/ifcn/
- MediaSmarts: www.mediasmarts.ca
- MediaWise: www.poynter.org/mediawise/
- News Literacy Project: www.newslit.org
- Teaching Kids News:
  www.teachingkidsnews.com/fakenews/

## Games

Some of the most effective tools are online games that teach you how journalism works, what fake news is and how to tell the difference.

- BBC iReporter: bbc.co.uk/news/resources/
  idt-8760dd58-84f9-4c98-ade2-590562670096
- Bad News (Junior): www.getbadnews.com/
  droggame_book/junior/#intro
- Doubt It or Trust It?: www.doubtit.ca/test-yourself/
- Fake or Foto?: www.area.autodesk.com/fakeorfoto
- FakeOut: www.newsliteracy.ca/fakeOut
- Poynter Institute: www.poynter.org/
  fact-checking/2019/want-to-be-a-better-fact
  -checker-play-a-game/
- Reality Check: mediasmarts.ca/sites/mediasmarts/
  files/games/reality-check/index.html#/
- Spot the Troll: www.spotthetroll.org/start

# ACKNOWLEDGMENTS

I'd like to thank my brilliant Teaching Kids News co-founders: Jon Tilly and Kathleen Tilly, who share my vision of helping kids know what's going on in the world, as well as Monique Conrod, Andrew Duncan and Valerie Strain.

Many people helped bring this book to life — first and foremost, my wonderful editor Kathleen "Structure Queen" Keenan who helped me organize my thoughts and who cares just as much as I do about fighting misinformation. My incredible agent, Jennifer Laughran, found this book a great home at Kids Can Press. Illustrator extraordinaire Kathleen Marcotte, designer Andrew Dupuis and production editor Olga Kidisevic made the book gorgeous. Thank you to media literacy experts Sam Wineburg (Stanford) and Matthew Johnson (MediaSmarts) for reviewing the book. Many journalist pals, including Angela Misri, John Lorinc, Colleen Ross, Irene Gentle and John Wells helped ensure the information is real-world and up-to-date.

Andrew and Bennett, always, for your love. Stephanie and Jane for your support. My mom, Heather, who will probably sell a lot of these books! And my writing groupers, Nicola, Karen B., Lana, Joe, Rebecca, Karen K. and Kari-Lynn as well as Nancy, Michelle and Gary. And WTW — cheer, cheer!

Lastly, thank you to you and all the other young people, educators, librarians and parents who care about reducing the spread of misinformation. It's not easy but it's incredibly important. Thank you for helping.

# GLOSSARY

**About page:** the page on a website that describes the website's purpose and intended audience, and sometimes says who created it

**advertorial:** an ad that is written and laid out to look like a news article

**artificial intelligence (AI):** a computer that can complete tasks, solve problems and learn in ways similar to the human brain

**bias:** the slant, outlook or prejudice through which a person views the world, stemming from their life experiences

**byline:** the name of the author who wrote an article

**correction:** an explanation of typos, errors or misleading information published in a news piece

**critical thinking:** the act of thinking about and questioning what you read and see, rather than just accepting it as true

**deepfake:** a misleading video that combines the audio from one with the visuals from another, usually to make it seem like someone is saying something they never said

**fact-checker:** a person whose job is to verify information in a news report

**headline:** a line at the top of an article or page that sums up or explains the text

**lede:** the first paragraph of a news story, usually containing the most important information

**opinion piece:** a news piece written or filmed specifically to persuade the audience to agree with the writer or broadcaster. May also be called an editorial or a column.

**photo credit:** the name of the photographer, usually found below or beside the image

**point of view:** the way a person looks at the world, based on their life experiences

**propaganda:** a form of fake news, usually about politics or world events, that is heavily biased or misleading and is designed to persuade the reader

**satire:** an exaggerated presentation of the facts in order to be humorous

**sensationalize:** to make something seem more exciting than it is, in order to attract attention and clicks

**skeptical:** being doubtful that something is as it seems

**social media:** digital platforms, such as Snapchat, YouTube, Instagram, Facebook, Twitter, TikTok and WhatsApp, where people share information, videos and images

**source:** the origin of information or facts. A source may be someone who has been interviewed in a news piece or it may be the publisher of a website.

**traffic:** viewership of, or clicks to, something online such as a website, post or video

**unbiased:** impartial or neutral

# INDEX